thank you for dreaming

poetry by

Jeannine M. Pitas

Dear Kent,
Thank you so much for your support.
Jeannine
January 12, 2019

©2018 Jeannine M. Pitas

All rights reserved. No part of this book may be reproduced without the express written permission of the author, except in the case of written reviews.

ISBN: 978-0-9984580-8-3

Library of Congress Control Number: 2018934095

First edition

PO Box 5301
San Pedro, CA 90733
www.lummoxpress.com

Printed in the United States of America

Acknowledgments

I am very grateful to Patric Nuttall for thoroughly reviewing several poems in this collection.

I am grateful to Hoa Nguyen, Sonia di Placido, Dale Easley, Rhonda Miska, Lauren K. Alleyne, Andrew Jones, Matt Muilenburg, Dan Cowper, Pat Connors and members of the Dubuque Area Writers' Guild for providing feedback on several of these poems. Thank you so much, RD Armstrong, for believing in me and encouraging my writing. Thanks to my family, friends, colleagues and students for the constant support.

Some poems from this collection have been published in *Labour of Love, Seedings Journal, Canthius, Presence, 3 Elements Review, U.S. Catholic, Lummox 6,* and the *Gallery* of the Dubuque Area Writers' Guild.

To M. Al Asker, H. Al Malak, and all you other falcons -

"No bird soars too high
if he soars with his own wings."
- William Blake

We Are One: An Introduction to *thank you for dreaming*

In this powerful collection of poems, Jeannine Pitas lays bare the wounds of our time—the fractures in our understanding and compassion, the heartache of loneliness, the dissonance between our instincts and actions, the general chaos of our technologically advanced, spiritually degraded societies. In an effort to treat those wounds, *thank you for dreaming* stands in defiance of boundaries and unnecessary demarcations of difference; whether it is "aging teachers, early-morning office cleaners, executives sitting alone on a million dollars," Frida Kahlo, Athena or God her/himself, the speaker of these poems reaches out in empathy and in love. These are poems in pursuit of connection that seek to bridge the distance between the past and the present, between knowing and mystery, between the secular and the sacred. Pitas traverses the internal worlds of the soul and the external world of politics, environment, and technology, and brings the two spheres into dialogue with each other. In "To an Immigrant," for example, the speaker repeats the line "I want to touch your life with mine," offering this intimate incantation as an alternative to xenophobia and hate, which she addresses head on in poems like "Just after my mother tells me she voted for Trump," in which she declares "Lady Liberty could have turned her back on us... She didn't." These are poems that urge us to give up the preconceived notions that hold us hostage in our own ignorance, wisely pointing out the limitations of such living:

> until I cross the river
> naked
> on a raft made of my own clothes
> what can I say I know
>   (the line)

They invite us again and again to participate in a radical reaching toward those who are different, disenfranchised, and dismissed, and show us how in so doing, we are engaging in our own healing. They give us new commandments through which we can live our most fruitful and fulfilling lives:

> don't lock your doors / don't let your eyes glaze in hours and hours of online delirium / don't bury yourself behind a mountain of books / go with your hands, eyes and ears open / go to listen and hold /

- Lauren K. Alleyne, author of *Difficult Fruit.*

How I Began

It's May 2006.
The streets are covered in autumn leaves

and I sit in a white-walled room
filled with people waiting for an answer.

Twenty-two and timid, I can't look my elders in the face
much less my youngers, or those the same age.

"What is your vision of Latin American literature?" they ask.
This is not my language; these are not my lands.

What am I supposed to say to these teachers
at the Centro Regional de Profesores in Salto, Uruguay?

I stare down at my hands, take a deep breath,
and, fumbling for words, I begin.

I speak of Neruda's fire on the wind,
of Gabriel García Márquez's winged old man.

I mention Borges' magnificent library
filled with all the selves we could ever hope to be.

I speak of Marosa di Giorgio's flaming garden,
Juan Rulfo's burning plain,

Ernesto Cardenal's prayers that the scales of the universe
might finally tip in the direction of justice.

I speak of Oscar Romero's martyrdom,
Mercedes Sosa's resounding thanks.

My voice takes off, no longer my own
as others speak through me.

And in that moment I know
from the Arctic to Tierra del Fuego

we are one America
india y del sol.

June 4, 1989

I wake up
the sun is shining
lilacs bloom on the branches
peonies teem with ants
beetles build a new world
under rocks

today is my birthday
my mother is making potato salad
my father is pulling out card tables and the grill
tonight there will be a party

at six years old
I feel I've lived forever
all this spring
I have checked the robins' blue eggs
in the nest they made outside our door
at Easter I held my Babcia's hand
wore the orchid corsage she gave me
a few weeks ago we visited Disney
I hugged Micky Mouse, kissed Minnie
visited replicas of Egypt and Mexico
believing all of it as real
as Mrs.Bova, my kindergarten teacher
as the crossing guard outside my school

today I help my mother dust the French doors
comb the fringe of Persian rugs
arrange a bouquet of silky roses
barely hearing the television's watery chatter

my world is garden walks with my father
Babcia's blue-pleated dresses, Mama's pancakes

still spring afternoons waiting for swallowtails
to land on the crease of my blouse

I do not know
that on another side of the earth
streets teem with people
shouting for joy
this day will be remembered
red and white, colors of the flag
as the moment when, after fifty years,
freedom returned to Poland

I do not know
that on still another side
Beijing's streets teem with people
screaming, fleeing
red and white, colors of blood and pale faces
filled with the worst kind of death –
a death preceded by fear
decades later, it will be mentioned in hushed tones –
the "June Fourth Incident"
that burns the backs of wordless throats

today is my birthday
I am turning six years old
relatives and friends gather to eat burgers
my mother is making potato salad
I open presents – Barbie dolls,
clothes, my first bicycle

I blow out the candles
on my Mickey Mouse cake
and wonder
what I should wish for

Father's Day

You made me.
As you took Mother's hand
placed the ring on her finger
you were already calling me

to be born in the season of light,
the time of turtles and strawberries,
bluegills and swallowtails,
the grace of lengthening June days.

As I grew, you pointed me to clear nights –
a crescent moon, Jupiter and Venus
aligned in orderly
rows of your making.

But you were also determined to show me disorder
as you turned on the television
to reveal rubber factories, exploding oil fields,
starving children. *This too is the world.*

Sometimes your love
was mixed with the smell of wine,
harsh words when I spilled pop
on the living room rug –

later, a shaking head, a curse
when I backed your car into the garage.
For some years you vanished,
left us on a train of double shifts

at the steel plant.
While you worked
sixteen hour days, Mother and I
ate our spaghetti or pork chops alone.

I did my homework, she read her Bible.
Without you, the tapping in the pipes
became footsteps of poltergeists
as your absence rapped against the walls.

I didn't yet know
that for you work meant love.
Today, you struggle to sit and stand,
to sleep through arthritic nights,

and spend afternoons dozing on the couch.
You can't walk through forests anymore.
You drive to the stream's edge,
watch younger men fish.

I know the time is coming –
like Aeneas I must carry you on my back
as you keep on mumbling
good advice I haven't requested

and exhort me to take the hands of others,
to hold them as you have held me.

American Gothic

She always knew she'd be the one
to care for her father in his old age.
No one has asked who will care for her.
She wears her mother's cameo, its pearly lady
stark against an oval the colour of diluted blood,
a shade different from the black of her dress,
the white of her house, the brown wheatfield
of the world she knows. At times she reads
Jane Austen, thinks of Marianne Dashwood yearning
for Willoughby, Liza Bennett finally united with her Darcy,
women with servants to plait their hair, wash their clothes.
For a while she had a canary, but one day, drunk,
her father unlatched the cage and cut its throat.
For a while, she sang in the church choir, but he made
her stop. "I need you here." Sometimes, while waiting
for the bread to rise, she remembers the lights of Chicago
she saw on her twentieth birthday when her aunt
took her to hear Irving Berlin; she remembers dancing
with the one high school boy who pretended to love her
before he joined the army and didn't come back.
She wears that pink and white cameo,
recalls the young girl she never was.
Her father eats the soup she makes, sips the
the beer she brews. They used to play
euchre, but now he just sits,
waiting for the winter
they both feel inside them.

Pearl

"Again, the kingdom of heaven is like a merchant seeking beautiful pearls, who, when he had found one pearl of great price, went and sold all that he had and bought it."
– Matthew 13: 45-46

To find a pearl.

The mollusk's afterlife glowing. A planet you might escape to, a place you could live. To see it in a jeweler's shop behind glass, to note the marked price. Exchange value. To resolve that this jewel is worth it. To sell all you have, make the deposit, go off and work for five years, seven. Day and night, day and night. To see that pearl when you look up at the moon, call it, whispering, *I need you, I love you, I'm coming for you soon.* Finally, to hold it in your hands. To kiss it, knowing it is more than an oyster's waste; it is an unbreakable husk that contains the sea's motion, the coral's pain, the starfish's hunger, the earth's determination to continue. It is the extinct ammonites and trilobites, barnacles, the watery world from which we have all come. It is our destiny, our darkness, our drowning. It is where the ship goes when it loses sight of the stars. To hold that pearl, resolving to do so for as long as you can.

To be a pearl.

Swept up by strange nets, snatched from your mother's red, life-giving warmth. To find yourself in a sterile, cold room where harsh lights reduce yours to the dullest glow, to realize you're not the round life you thought you were. Here, you are placed among other gleaming lives and nonlives, new homes extracted from earth and sea. To be locked in a false, man-made mollusk, a strange glass husk that refuses to break. Until you see that every day, other eyes come to meet you – large, human eyes that remind you of the sun as it looked from beneath the sea. To trust those eyes, understanding they belong to a new mother, one who will lead you to a place of safety, a moment of union and melding, a new kind of sea. To quell your pain, find hope in your days. To grow larger and stronger under that welcome gaze. To look at your companions – amethysts, rubies – and notice their lustre. To wonder where they came from, to imagine ideas of how you will get out, be touched again by the sun, fit your natural shape, shine as you know you were meant to.

To find a pearl.

To pass the jeweler's window day after day and look at it. To admire its beauty and contemplate buying it. To walk the streets in frustration, desire for that white light that contains all colors. Exchange value. The price is too high. To imagine breaking into the store at night and stealing it. Crazy thoughts. But purchase seems impossible. You'd have to sell everything just to make the deposit. Five, seven years you'd work. Early mornings, late nights. Living on little. To watch others marry, take out mortgages and buy cars while you throw your life away for a jewel. To hear their voices echoing in your ears: *It isn't worth it.* To decide they must be right. To think tenderly from time to time, to wonder who claimed it in the end, then push that thought from your mind. To move on. Live your life.

To be a pearl.

To grow dependent on those twin suns that shine toward you each day. To yearn for them. To need them, call them. One day, to find them gone. To perk up, searching. Where are they? To realize they aren't coming back. There is no way out for you. You are not as pure, as exquisite, as luminous as you wanted to be. You no longer gleam. You could be any material – plastic beneath artificial lights. Your price is lowered. Exchange value. Eventually someone buys you. You are stored away in the casket of a jewelry box. For years you imagine those eyes returning, seeking you. They don't. You are moved from darkness to darkness. One day, months or centuries later, you find yourself surrounded by water. Dropped in a ditch, flushed down a toilet, transported by someone who does not know what you once were. Suddenly it is warm. You remember your mother, your grandmother, your sisters and brothers on the waves. They are near you. You see the sun, brighter than those two eyes ever could have been. You fall into the waves, the foam. You are radiant; you are radiance. You are light.

Augustine's Lover

Lord, grant me chastity and continence, but not yet.

– Augustine of Hippo

It's said that she converted first,
abandoning their bed
more readily than he did.
That sounds like a tale
a man might tell.

Did she beg, plead,
stare at the wall, roll her eyes
while little Adeodatus
clung to her skirts?

Did she gather up his robes
and fling them into the dusty street?
Did she beg him to stay with her,
at least meet up every other Thursday
among the stench of the root cellar?

For fifteen years his un-wife, shadow,
lurid secret – until *agape* displaced *eros*.
He was ready to marry an invisible
being – not the mother of his child.

Did she shake her head at this narcissist?
Jesus, the one who commanded men
to leave wives, children behind,
eat with sinners and tax collectors,
who dismissed his mother at Cana,
"Woman, what have I to do with thee?"

Perhaps she'd known this day would come.
She would have to disappear
once he tried to become all soul
and no body, even though,
observing her first wrinkles,
he could feel his own skin's sagging.

Oh Holy Augustine!
Illustrious Warrior against the Foes of the Church!
Inexhaustible Fountain of Christian Eloquence!
Pillar of the True Faith!
Tell me who got cast aside
when you became a saint.

I'd canonize her myself,
wear her medal around my neck,
pray for her intercession,
call her patroness of single mothers,
abandoned lovers...
She – not he – my guardian.

I'd pull her from the dusty shelves
of the abandoned libraries,
etch her into a thousand
stained glass windows,
sculpt her into a statue,
lift her for all to see –

If only I knew
her name

Dido

*"What has love of land given to you
that I have not?"*

    – HD, "The Islands"

Tell me
what is piety
but a justification for breaking?

It seemed easy enough.
Juno promised me
a new kingdom – no, a queendom
never before seen

then gathered branches, built
a bed that looked like a nest
(I did not know it was a net)
where she sang your will into my ear.

What could love of land give me
that you could not?
Maybe I could have both –
"and" is the golden contrast
to the grayness of "or."

Beauty came from the sea.
My city's coast received your ships,
its inlets stilling them with a promise.

Your skin, so fragile, orchids I yearned
to water, held war concealed,
conquest in the plunge of soft belly,
pollen-dusted rage.

Yes, I know you're a man
who believes in razor-sharp "or," not
the softer "and..." But what do you expect
to gain from love of land?

Beauty coated me, sticky, singing –
what trick, what night, what limit.
I know you're turning your head to look
at my city's smoke and flame.

I know you're still going to see me
long after your ship sails away.

Frida

Gorgeous, freedom-seeking Frida, those weren't dreams you
 painted.
I see you with your flowers, the black hairs of your head and
 body, determined

to prove that your face could hold as much history
as any mural, that your eyes contain the gaze of thousands, that
 your hair could

grow long, back to a time before your people were labeled *una
 raza cósmica.*
Frida, holding hands with yourself, determined to paint your
 way through

Diego's great form. You didn't need him but took him anyway,
 tattooed him
on your forehead, donned his suit, asked him to hold you, to see
 you. But he didn't,

and neither do we, as we transform you into our chic Day of the
 Dead cover girl,
our secular Guadalupe, Mexican Marilyn Monroe, poster child
 for love addicts

and accident victims, as we set you on the altar with Sylvia,
Virginia, all the other crazy women artists

we forget that what we coo and smile at
is your lifelong fight to be seen.

Magdalene

I did not waver at the sight of him.
A beloved apostle, I clung to the wood of the cross,
refused to avert my eyes.

Where the mind dwells, there lives the treasure.
While the rest of you ran away and hid,
I, determined, waited.

Later, envious, you refused to believe
in my testament of the empty tomb,
my faith that our beloved walked again.

You did not stone me,
but sent me off
to speak with stones,

beauty rent with a thought
for the thrust of the sword,
a fat pope's word.

Five hundred years later, Gregory
called me a prostitute, or else the sister
of Lazarus, or maybe his mother.

My message is the same: Hell is no worse
than the world you are making
as you tune out the news that could have saved you

and tear the flowers out of the earth.
If you need me, I'll be in the place called barren
where my deathless beloved brings forth water

from rocks, transforms it into wine,
where I make treasures from my mind –
the truest promised land.

Those of you now called prophets
will come, like me, to be known as sinners –
Like me, you'll speak of resurrection and not be believed.

My roots drag color from sand,
my rivulets flow with gold,
and you'll remember the beloved apostle.

But the desert is vaster than your mind can imagine.
So go on. I dare you.
Try and find me.

Tracing Us

Our meeting was common.
You were sitting at the bar
when I drifted in from an afternoon
amid fleeting cherry blossoms, April pink.

But before that? Winter.
Surely we both traipsed
around the city in heavy coats,
grumbling in the subway.

Did I ever pass you in the street?
Did I duck in front of you to enter
a crowded bus? Did I toss my bag
on the seat that should have been yours?

Then, autumn.
Making your home here, you navigated
through immigration offices and costumes,
adult learning centres, jack-o-lanterns.

Meanwhile I wept
in a psychologist's office
beside the man I loved
when said he could no longer love me.

Before that? Summer.
You landed in my country
on the day of the parade.
Amid fireworks and majorettes

you unpacked your suitcase
in a tiny apartment shared with your parents
while I read Robert Graves at the beach
and wondered why life felt so wrong.

Before that, it gets harder to trace.
There's an ocean between me
and my understanding of you
until I return to 2003, when,

at nineteen
I saw boys my age
get shipped off
to invade your country.

I watched bombs fall on prime-time TV –
"Shock and awe," we called it.
Somewhere in that city you were hiding
between the flimsy walls of your house

barricaded by the dreamscapes
of old movies –
Rita Hayworth, Sophia Loren,
Marilyn Monroe, smiling muses.

You sketched, painted,
played the oud,
creation your best resistance
to the sirens.

Sometimes you dreamed
of walking free through safe streets,
gazing at a clean blue sky.
You always woke up.

I want to go back
to a time before war,
numbers, money, oil,
even before prayer.

I picture us, three years old in our gardens,
me with my maple trees,
you with your palms.
Both of us smile as we play tag with cousins,

chase butterflies, leaf through the pages
of books we can't read yet,
draw pictures of a world
like us, still unbroken.

thank you for dreaming

you tell me of your dream
in which Muhammad appeared

surrounded by imams
he shined in your family's garage

you speak of the time
when God broke his own law

showed his enormous face
and drank tea with your mother

oh, dreamer
you have enchanted me

with songs
of your beloved Babylon

laughter at Charlie Chaplin
your best resistance to war

memories of licorice,
yucca, Jericho roses in bloom

now, after escaping
the tortures and amputations

you have made it to safety
with your hands intact –

you will use them
to play the oud

you have made it to freedom
with your tongue intact –

you will use it
to tell your stories

you have made it to this adopted country
with your heart intact

and you will use it to find people
like you, once silenced –

touched and held
by your dreams

To an Immigrant

I want to touch your life with mine.
To accompany you in the Halloween pumpkin carvings,
Thanksgiving dinners, the festooning of windows
with Christmas lights. Photographs let me glimpse you,
follow you down winter, summer streets
as your dark eyes reach to touch the camera's light.
You've known the emptiness in a child's cry, the
din of falling bombs, nights spent hiding in a desert village,
days crumpled in the trunk of a car before boarding a plane
bound for place you never thought you'd live.
I want to touch your life with mine, let my hand clasp
your pictures' corners, rummage through dollar stores in search of
orange masks, bake October pumpkin pie, pour December
wine, help you transform this labyrinth
of ads and holidays into a home.

the line

until I cross the river
naked
on a raft made of my own clothes
what can I say I know

until I emerge
from that cold water
and see the flashing red, white and blue
flag of a police car

until I fall in love at fifteen
and end up two years later alone
with twin boys
I can't afford to feed

until I've spent so many nights
looking up at the moon while they sleep
and wonder if my mother
might possibly still see us

until I've stood in more lines
than I ever knew existed, lost in a
maze of offices
the papers enough to bury me

until I hear the megaphone at 3 a.m.
feel the cold metal of handcuffs around me
get led away in my pajamas
as my children cry in the arms of another

until I cross the river
naked
on a raft made of my own clothes
what can I say I know

Just after my mother tells me she voted for Trump

At forty, you cringed as your boss
told "dumb Polak" jokes on the phone
behind the half-closed door of his office.
Clenching, you repeated the litany you'd learned –
Marie Curie, *we are not stupid,*
Frédéric Chopin, *we are not stupid.*

Today, you remember how your own mother
ironed underwear, washed porches, sold shoes
at the downtown department store,
saved for a house of her own,
and mirrored the picket-fenced manners
of those she wished to become.

Just after you tell me
we need to protect our borders
I ask why you sent me to the Polish Saturday School
to conjugate verbs and learn of uprisings
in a place you'd never seen
if "American" has no room for hyphens.

And when you say "Our ancestors learned English,"
I just ask that you recall your own Babcia's subscription
to the *Daily Dziennik,* her refusal
to speak anything but her native tongue
until she died.

Lady Liberty could have turned her back on us
as she has done many times. She didn't.
The Ellis Island we take photos of
was a detention and deportation center
that we – but not all – escaped from.

*America First, American carnage, make America
great again, pass the ban build the wall,*
Mama, Mamusia, tell me –
Where on earth do you think we came from?
Who the hell can we say we are?

Macondo

Once, a village lost its memory.
The people hung two signs to remind themselves of the facts:
"This is Macondo" and "God exists."

Day and night bled together, moonlit midnight
shone bright as noon, midday sun
looked like midnight under the blue.

They lost but didn't know they were losing.
They died, but some returned from death
unable to bear the solitude.

They tried to take photographs of God
and proved the world was orange-round
centuries after everyone else knew.

Priests walked across the sky;
strange children appeared on doorsteps –
like stray dogs, all were taken in.

The town was a cloth made of
Amaranta's constant sewing,
cloth seamed crookedly with unwept tears.

Sometimes, a war broke out.
Sometimes a man faced a firing squad
and survived.

This is the pantheon in my attic's photographs,
staring unsmiling into a future
from which their names have been erased.

This is the catalogue of gray names,
facelessly engraved into a plaque
on the wall of St. Stanislaus Church.

I imagine them rising each morning,
men bound for the steel plant, women
off to mend socks and iron sheets.

I'm trying to work as they did,
to keep the floors swept, the shelves full of books,
to rejoice in the sewing of shrouds.

I'm trying to pray as they did,
not to be surprised when a child
becomes a feather and floats into the sky.

To let words fly off, yellow butterflies
on wind, never expecting them to return,
but welcoming them when they do.

To dance and fight and study
Melquiades' parchments
before I, too, lose both name and face.

Amaranta

A woman made with the taste of almonds,
you fell from a tree believed wrongly to be sweet.

You imagined your thoughts could make pools of poison
appear in your niece Remedios's coffee, your red envy casting
a gray haze over the village your parents founded.

Your queendom, the porch, where you sewed and sewed in a
house without men. You raised the children of others, a spider
turned from in horror, your web the home in which others
could live.

When your nephew Aureliano touched you, your yearning was
wider than war, harsher than the banana company. It threatened
to raze the whole village, give birth to a child with the tail of a
pig.

Yearning to rise up and fly as only priests and idiots can, you
raised a wall between self and desire, shut your bedroom door
forever, collected letters to bear to the dead.

Virgin sacrifice, widow of no one, you closed your nostrils to
the smell of lavender, your ears to the strains of the pianola,
sent suitors away from the porch where you ruled.

For years you sat, weaving your own shroud, Penelope with no
Odysseus to wait for. You sought the God your father lost faith
in, strove to take a photograph of love and hold it.

I see you in so many aging teachers, early-morning office
cleaners, executives sitting alone on a million dollars. I see you
and wish to seek you, sit on the porch beside you, walk in the
sun and hold out your thread.

I'd ask your almond-shell to surround us like an autumn day, let us drink the dark chocolate that grants eternal life, let others fly or stay behind walls or go to war or pick the imperialists' bananas

as we sit on this porch and spin stories, weave of them a flimsy web, making and unmaking our Macondos before the dustclouds will at last call us home.

Athena

Long ago
before corporations received
human rights
before the British Empire struggled
to stop the sunset
before the telescope and microscope
extended our sight
there was Athena –

her arrows sharper
than those of Eros
she guided Odysseus
around Circe and Kalypso's islands
kept him safe
from Poseidon's mess of blue motion.

Long ago
before a group of long-robed men
devised all questions and answers
needed to get to heaven
before witches were burned
before the prison shined its searchlights
perpetually unclosed eyes
there was Athena –

putting Clytaemnestra in her place
she refused
to let the red-black
Furies avenge the queen's death
turned them into silent
seers, an imaginary jury.

Athena, beloved of male heroes and gods
angel of reason
a woman who never experienced
the inconveniences of being born
giving birth
dying –

One day in the twenty-first Century
at the Machine Intelligence Research Institute
a group of men
set out to rebuild her –
They selected a Zeus
sliced his brain like a pineapple
photographed it onto a computer
and waited for her to emerge.

They cut off her shield
removed her garments
swelled her to four times her size
distilled her wisdom into another program
made thousands of copies
to sell to CEOs.

They did not listen
when she started to scream,
they did not notice
when she writhed.
Trapped on their electronic
mountain, she wept at the knowing
she was just a woman
after all –

La Llorona

I am not la Virgen de Guadalupe, that praying goddess
in blue and pink, cocooned by spikes, a yellow fence.
For hours I knelt before her image, asked her what
made her demand a church built in her name.
She pretends to give without taking – she hears our prayers
and stands on them like those roses beneath her feet,
lets our cancer and heartbreak and unpaid bills adorn her.
I tried to live in such unlaughing, unweeping compassion,
a love that pretends to ask nothing from no one.

I am not la Malinche, the conquistador's interpreter,
America's original Eve. In the painting she rides
with Cortés on his horse, every little girl's fantasy
of growing up beautiful, desired, loved, not knowing
that so often they'll end up *chingada*, remade into an instrument
for the use of some man. I wonder how she felt as her people's
temples were looted, women and children enslaved, thousands
of years of history erased. I too have painted futures
from the blue, green, brown watercolors
of men's eyes, crystal palaces from their light.
But really I have nothing a conquistador would take.

Instead, I'd be la Llorona, that weeping mother who,
enraged, drowned her children to spite the man
who betrayed her. Like her I'll walk the earth, struggling
to believe I'll find them, not accepting I've drowned
the beloved future that came out of me.
La Virgen stares down in compassionate reproach,
La Malinche looks up and laughs,
as I walk and walk with my graveyard flowers,
begging the singer to give me mercy, hoping
one day I'll return to heaven
and find a door ajar.

The Last Horse

*And this horse with a mane the color of seafoam
is the first horse the world has ever seen.*

— Gwendolyn MacEwan

The last horse the world will ever see
stands and watches
across this street of endless sunlight.

I stare, wondering how I'm going to tell it
about shrapnel, phosphorous bombs,
all the broken countries it has never known.

This horse does not know
that others like it
have disappeared from this place,
replaced by steel and oil that claim its power.

It does not know
that sunlit fields and cardinals and rivers
were squeezed and reshaped
into highways, drainpipes, hot dogs.

It's looking at me,
waiting for some explanation
of where to go, how to fit.

I look upward, point to the sun,
that one god we can't touch,
giver of life that touches us, last lord.

I want to turn toward it and say go, leave,
fly back to wherever you came from,
you're not safe, we will hurt you here.

But it's too late.
My silence has given permission,
and the horse has moved away from me.

It's trotting away, turning
into an alley between the high rises.
I break inside: Wait.

The System

The system shines with uninterrupted light.

— Lisa Robertson

There is grass and clouds and blenders stirring morning mango smoothies.

There is the Brooklyn Bridge and Union Square with Hare Krishnas singing to their drums, buskers reciting Shakespeare, children rushing to break enormous bubbles blown by a machine.

There are subways and rats and robotic voices apologizing for delays, chocolate shops with crystal chandeliers and shiny glass surfaces, would-be witches gathering herbs in Prospect Park while drones deliver parcels over their heads.

There are protesters occupying building sites and drivers rolling their eyes at them and more protesters offering roses to riot police.

There are women disappearing from the streets of Vancouver, evicted men roaming San Francisco while Googleati ride by in private buses.

There are gold coins in vaults and gold crosses hanging around the necks of Fox News commentators and miners digging into Incan soil while Goldcorps goes up a few more points on the Toronto Stock Exchange, while Xiomara looks out the window and cries no, *I beg you, please, not my water..*

There are late Renoirs and replicas of ancient Egyptian temples and Scotiabank-sponsored surtitles at the Canadian Opera Company's *Rigoletto.*

There are trays and trays of plastic water bottles at every academic conference in every windowless hotel banquet hall, bus maps and Gothic revival churches dwarfed by skyscrapers; there are gods and there is God and how are any of us supposed to know the difference.

There are steel mills and "men working" signs and stone-faced men and women in the waiting rooms of HIV testing centres; there are garbage continents in the Pacific and Ghanian valleys filled with broken cell phones, businessmen sipping cocktails in Grand Central before catching the train back to Scarsdale; turquoise beads hanging from garlands in the shops; there are big box stores and weeping statues, heaven and hell squeezed down to the size of a single tree; there are vans painted in William Blake drawings and underwater grids containing all the parts of ourselves we'd rather not have to see.

There is toxic forgiveness floating like smog around those who haven't asked for it; there is the Bloor Viaduct hand-built by the old dispossessed, now guarded by high fences to keep the new dispossessed from jumping off.

Is there any border, any ring, any outside to this system that holds us, this net that economists deem beautiful? An edge to the web that contains us like flies, a wormhole we might crawl through to another planet locked inside ours, waiting to burst into leaf? Is there a way to find the sea in the reflection of a building, to look up and see the sun?

I see disasters and tears and gated communities patrolled by labradoodles; I see hatred in the shape of beauty, an onion of crystal ice.

I see apartments and buzzers and kitchens and floors, groups of people scribbling post-it notes with the names of the famous and pasting them to their foreheads, an endless party game where we sip our wine and eat our brie and ask each other who we are.

A Prayer

After Rainer Maria Rilke

Pray, God.
I will hear you.

I stare at the dawn-lit river's waves,
waiting for you to speak.

Your head is covered
with footprints.

It must hurt, the steps of people
who walk over you, the motorcycles engines,

the church bells and constant *azan*, the whispers
of rosaries and screams from playgrounds

and weeping from burning cities combined
into a dissonant, enormous sound.

Perhaps, like Beethoven, you struggle
to sing the world from sounds you've lost.

You reach for them the way an old man tries to remember
his grandmother rocking him, singing,

the way we try to remember
the first moment something tore the night,

a hole of light in dark cloth, a peephole we look through
for eighty years, or sixty, or maybe just twenty-seven.

Tomorrow I resolve to help you; I will wake up
early in the pink dawn, stay up late into the night, window

open, ear pressed to the sky. I will stand on my balcony
above the taxis' horns, the shouts from Manhattan streets,

the lush soundscape of a grassy summer field.
Pray, God. I will listen.

Mandatum Novum

for years I refused / to wear your sign / I knew they'd look at me /
and see the clash of swords / burning cities / children shaking
in their beds on Saturday nights / afraid of the Sunday morning
sacristy / Torquemada's tortures / Galileo's angry assertion /
"And yet it moves" / looking at me / they'd see a city covered in
gold / turned away from millions / of Lazaruses begging at its
gates / they'd hear cries of "sinner" / to those whose love
is deemed unclean / they'd hear shouts of "murderer" / to the
rape victim / just too damn tired / of being a mother to pain /
they'd see residential schools / smallpox blankets / Christopher
Columbus using the Bible / to sanction his lust / for gold /
Bartolomé de las Casas, protector of the Indians / who, full
of good intentions, decreed the Middle Passage / a road to
freedom/

if they saw your sign around my neck / I know they'd not hear /
Oscar Romero's desperate cries / *Cesa la represión* / they'd
not hear Dorothy Day's assertion / that the answer / to the long
loneliness / is community / they'd not hear the call / to feed the
hungry / visit the imprisoned / pray for the living and the dead /
they'd not see the thousands / gathered outside the gates / of the
military base / urging those inside / to study war no more /

but I have seen / the thief forgiven / I have watched / the
homeless meth addict / get offered a bed / I have heard your
voice / in the Fauré Requiem in Oxford / *la misa campesina* in
Nicaragua / *candombe* drumming in Uruguayan Streets / and
I've finally decided / to wear the instrument / of your execution /
you, who knew you would die / for a crime you did not commit /
you who, on your final night / turned to us and said / take my
body / drink my blood / bind it to your own / and then go /

into the broken oceans / go into the burning forest / replaced by fields of soy / go into the cities / where men stand alone on balconies / move among the night walkers / who weave their way through construction sites / go to the pipelines, swim through the black ink / you've used to write your names on this land / don't lock your doors / don't let your eyes glaze in hours and hours of online delirium / don't bury yourself behind a mountain of books / go with your hands, eyes and ears open / go to listen and hold /

Resurrections

I am not done with my changes.

    – *Stanley Kunitz*

Do you remember the moment this morning
when your patch of earth turned to face the sun
and drops of light flooded your bedroom?

Do you remember last February's crocuses,
white and purple flags claiming winter's
landscape as their own?

Do you remember your own deaths, rosaries
entwined through your fingers, relatives keening over
your body, the coffins that shut you in darkness?

Do you remember when your First Communion
and wedding dresses were ripped, when your
prayer books and diplomas were torn?

Do you remember your Confirmation
when the bishop placed his hands on your forehead,
sealed your skin with oil, ordered you to receive the Holy Spirit?

Do you remember when the machines we made
began to speak, when we realized the world
had always been conscious?

Do you remember your first hajj, the spiral sea
of pilgrims in white as you let yourself
become a wave?

Do you remember when the last monarch butterfly
landed on milkweed and opened her wings,
determined to keep loving the sun?

Do you remember the first foreign language
you learned, words like the kisses of
a patient lover, rejoicing and blessed to touch you?

Do you remember when you released helium balloons,
watched them get smaller and smaller against the pink November
sky, believed they would reach the moon's crescent?

You cannot remember it all.
You fold and unfold as autumn becomes winter,
as spring drags you back into newness –

Do you remember the moment this morning
when your patch of earth turned to face the sun,
when drops of light flooded your bedroom?

Mary Comes Down

It is said
she was assumed into heaven.
Deathless, she stood on the moon,
was crowned with twelve stars.

But today in Rome I see her
begging outside the stone churches
that hold her statue.

In Jordan she sleeps in a refugee camp,
invites neighbors for tea,
shoots a film of her kids' pick-up soccer games –
(she's heard that in the West
they like this sort of thing).

In the San Fernando valley
she bends to harvest grapes,
she cuts garlic and gets half
the wages she was promised.

In Mexico she sells lace
and tells anyone who will listen
that four of her sons
have disappeared from Veracruz.

In Iowa, she sweeps the floor at Walmart
after the other workers have left.
Before this, she worked in a slaughterhouse.
Her task: to kill the male chicks.

She who once deflected
the Plague's sharpest arrows
now tends to those dying of AIDS
in a Kenyan village.

Sometimes she makes the news
when her raft capsizes on the Mediterranean,
but it goes unnoticed
when she is sold into slavery,
dies in childbirth,
walks for a day to fetch water,
and finds the well dry.

Again and again
her son offers to raise her,
adorn her in royal blue,
a final glorious mystery.

Again and again
she shakes her head,
gives the diadem back,
casts off her mantel
to cover a child.

Jeannine M. Pitas is the author of two previous poetry chapbooks: *A Place to Go* (Toronto: Lyricalmyrical Press, 2015) and *Our Lady of the Snow Angels* (Lyricalmyrical Press, 2012). She is also the Spanish-English translator of *I Remember Nightfall* (Ugly Duckling Presse, 2017), a collection of four books by acclaimed Uruguayan poet Marosa di Giorgio. She teaches at the University of Dubuque in Iowa.

The LUMMOX Press was established in 1994
by the poet, RD Armstrong.
Previous publications include the Little Red Book series
and the Lummox Journal. Currently publishing
chapbooks, a perfect bound poetry series,
a Poetry Anthology & Poetry Contest (annually),
and "e-copies" (PDFs) of most books.

The goal of the press and its publisher is to
raise the bar for poetry, while bringing
the "word" to an international audience.
We are proud to offer this book
as part of that effort.

For more information and to see our
growing catalog, please go to
www.lummoxpress.com

Made in the USA
Lexington, KY
03 January 2019